S0-ATV-175

Silverton School Library
1160 Snowden
Box 128
Silverton, CO 81433

GLOBALIZATION

Essential Viewpoints

GLOBALIZATION
BY SARA M. HAMILTON

Content Consultant
Bob Wood, Professor of Sociology
Rutgers University, Camden Campus

ABDO
Publishing Company

CREDITS

Published by ABDO Publishing Company, 8000 West 78th Street, Edina, Minnesota 55439. Copyright © 2009 by Abdo Consulting Group, Inc. International copyrights reserved in all countries. No part of this book may be reproduced in any form without written permission from the publisher. The Essential Library™ is a trademark and logo of ABDO Publishing Company.

Printed in the United States.

Editor: Jill Sherman
Copy Editor: Paula Lewis
Interior Design and Production: Nicole Brecke
Cover Design: Nicole Brecke

Library of Congress Cataloging-in-Publication Data
Hamilton, Sara M.
  Globalization / by Sara M. Hamilton.
     p. cm. — (Essential viewpoints)
  Includes bibliographical references and index.
  ISBN 978-1-60453-109-1
  1. Globalization. I. Title.

JZ1318.H346 2009
303.48'2—dc22

                        2008006995

TABLE OF CONTENTS

U'wa live in the Andes Mountains in Colombia.

WHAT IS GLOBALIZATION?

igh up in the mountains of Colombia, South America, an indigenous tribe named the U'wa has lived for thousands of years. Until the 1970s, they had almost no contact with the outside world. The U'wa believe they were put on this earth to keep the world in harmony. They are entirely self-sufficient and make use of everything from their natural habitat. Leaves serve as plates. Vines are used as bowstrings. Certain roots are used for medicinal purposes. The U'wa once thrived in a large region of Colombia. But over the years, the tribe has retreated farther into the Andes Mountains to avoid contact with the outside world.

Approximately 100 miles (160 km) east of the mountains is the Caño Limon oil field. It is licensed to international oil corporations. Both the Anglo-Dutch-owned Shell and the U.S.-owned Occidental (Oxy) corporations operate there. Approximately 1.2 billion barrels of oil are pumped from the field every day. The Caño Limon oil preserves are expected to be depleted within ten years. With the available oil dwindling, Shell and Oxy began looking for new oil fields in the region. They discovered that the territory of Samore has nearly as much oil as Caño Limon. Shell and Oxy sought to move in—but the U'wa, who inhabited much of the land, protested.

"I sing the traditional songs to my children. I teach them that everything is sacred and linked. How can I tell Shell and Oxy that to take the petrol is for us worse than killing your own mother? If you kill the earth, then no one will live. I do not want to die. Nobody does. No, it is not a gesture."[1]
—D., daughter of a wedhaiya, U'wa tribe

To the U'wa, oil represents the blood of Mother Earth. To drain the blood would kill the land and cause imbalance in the world. Many of the U'wa were prepared to die for this belief. In protest, they threatened to hurl themselves off a remote and sacred cliff, the Cliff of Death. A tribesman, Berichá Kubar'uwa, explained,

> *The communities will die. We can't give permission to develop oil. You can't sell Mother Moon. We don't even sell our timber or cattle, so why would we want to try to sell the blood of Mother Earth? . . . The government will sit down with us to see how we can live with Oxy and their oil exploration in our territory, without our culture being destroyed. But for us, this is impossible.* [2]

But it was not just the beliefs of the U'wa that were being threatened. In Colombia, oil fields often attract thousands of displaced people—and guerrilla warfare. Colombia has had periods of civil and guerrilla warfare. Its two main guerrilla groups, ELN and FARC, continue to operate in Colombia. Since Shell and Oxy arrived, these groups have caused hundreds of murders, massacres, tortures, and kidnappings. In addition, a 372-mile (599-km) oil pipeline runs from Caño Limon to the coastline.

The pipeline has been bombed hundreds of times in the past 20 years, as guerrilla forces try to exert their control over the region. These bombings contributed to a loss of 1.5 million barrels of oil and irreparable damage to the environment. The presence of guerrilla groups in Caño Limon is a dangerous threat to the U'wa.

The U'wa wanted no part in developing oil fields in Samore. Although they were offered financial compensation by Shell and Oxy, they refused. While the U'wa had rights to the land, they did not possess rights to its minerals. The Colombian government was in a difficult situation. Its constitution demanded protection of all indigenous tribes. Yet oil was its largest export and brought billions of dollars into the country. The dispute was brought to Colombia's highest court. The court sided with Shell and Oxy and gave them the right to drill in Samore.

Fortunately, the U'wa did not have to face the ultimate sacrifice at the Cliff of Death. Shell

"Occidental is committed to operating its business in a manner that respects the prevailing legal, cultural and social norms in the areas where we operate. We strive to minimize our operational impact and provide sustainable community benefits that will improve the quality of life for the residents while enabling the communities to assume the responsibility for their own development in a way that preserves the traditional cultural values."[3]
—*Occidental Oil Web site*

and Oxy withdrew their plans to drill in Samore, saying there was no oil there. But the Colombian government still has the legal right to sell the U'wa tribe's mineral-rich land at any time. This type of change could bring an end to the U'wa's way of life.

The story of the U'wa is just one effect of globalization. This term has been used only within the last few decades, but it is a concept that has been around for much longer.

A New Term

Over the years, the concept of globalization has gained more public attention and debate. Even the term *globalization* has had its share of controversy. Many falsely believe that Theodore Levitt, a professor at the Harvard Business School, coined the term *globalization* in a 1983 article he wrote for the *Harvard Business Review* titled, "The Globalization of Markets." In the article, Levitt wrote that advances in technology and changing social behaviors would have a drastic effect on international business—globalizing the world. In the weeks following its publication, more than 35,000 reprints were produced. *Harvard Business Review* estimates that approximately 850,000 copies of the article have been reproduced as of 2006.

Although Levitt greatly contributed to the widespread usage of the term, some believe *globalization* was first used as early as 1944. There is also evidence that the term was published throughout the 1980s in various economic papers, before Professor Levitt's article.

WHAT IS GLOBALIZATION?

In very broad terms, globalization is the worldwide integration of economic, technological, political, cultural, and social aspects between countries. Often the term

Occidental Petroleum wanted to drill for oil in Samore, Colombia.

is used when referring to economic globalization. Economic globalization involves trading and investing between countries. Trade is a driving force behind international relations. Trade impacts nearly every aspect of society.

For example, one of Colombia's primary exports in trade is oil. Large corporations such as Shell and Oxy establish businesses in the country to export the oil. This provides jobs for Colombian citizens. The Colombian government also receives money from these businesses in the form of taxes. The

Colombian government plays a role in establishing policies and trade agreements with other countries. These trade agreements could help Colombia in international politics and give the nation more leverage in policies. Or, if the trade agreements are unfair, they could damage Colombia's international reputation. Colombia's oil industry may provide more jobs and greater wealth, but it also has the potential to destroy cultures and damage the environment. Globalization seldom is a clear-cut, black-and-white issue.

The Heart of the Controversy

Globalization is not a new phenomenon. But within the last few decades, the advances made in technology, international trade, and communication have soared. Such a dramatic shift into a globalized world has led many to question the benefits and pitfalls of globalization.

The increase in trade, as well as technological, communication, and transportation advancements, have allowed societies to become more connected. What people eat, what movies they watch, and even what values they share have become more similar across borders. This may create a common bond between nations and cultures, but it may also breed an increase in nationalism, terrorism, or loss of culture.

BENEFITS

Those who favor globalization view it as a means by which countries may develop economically and increase their standard of living. International trade through globalization can have many benefits. Trade helps increase economic wealth and establishes good political relationships with trading partners. Globalization also promotes free trade and competition between corporations. This gives consumers throughout the world more options and cheaper products from which to choose.

Proglobalists, as supporters of globalization are sometimes called, believe that globalization increases employment and allows for more efficient uses of resources. In the long run, this helps the environment. In this way, globalization can

Views on Globalization

In a 2007 report from the Pew Global Attitudes Project, a survey of more than 45,000 people in 47 countries revealed that the majority believe international trade benefits their countries. However, the survey also indicated that the people are increasingly concerned about the negative aspects of globalization as well.

Support for international corporations and a global economy is decreasing somewhat in America and Europe. In contrast, countries in Asia, including China and India, report widespread approval. Despite approval of a global economy, these nations are wary of politically dominant nations.

help reduce poverty and give developing nations an opportunity to grow economically. They also believe globalization helps advance civil liberties, democracy, and human rights throughout the world.

Drawbacks

Although there may be many benefits to globalization, it can also have damaging effects on countries worldwide. One major drawback of globalization is the frequency with which developed countries exploit developing nations through free-trade agreements. In addition, some people view globalization as the Westernization or Americanization of the world. They say that these influences overtake a country's traditional identity.

Because of globalization, opponents argue, workers are exploited. The working conditions are poor, and the workers receive meager wages. The spread of industry to developing nations also has damaging effects on the environment. International corporations often take advantage of lax environmental regulations in these areas. Although globalization is often seen as a way to improve the standard of living, it has been a major factor in increasing the gap between the rich and the poor. This gap has widened both within nations and between developed and developing countries.

The Middle Ground

Although there are many who are either for or against globalization, there are countless others who fall somewhere in the middle. For many, globalization is neither inherently good nor bad. The vast majority of people recognize that globalization has many benefits but also recognize that there are many important drawbacks that need to be addressed. For example, some may view the increase of cultural interaction as being beneficial but worry that international corporations are harming the environment. Similarly, others may recognize that there are drawbacks to certain laws and agreements surrounding free trade but still feel that globalization has the potential to help developing countries.

The vast majority of globalization's critics and proponents

"Globalization is a set of beliefs that fosters a sense of connectivity, interdependence, and integration in the world community. It highlights commonalities without overlooking differences, and it extends benefits and responsibilities on a global scale."[4]
—*Abbas J. Ali, professor and executive director of the American Society for Competitiveness*

stand somewhere within this middle ground. Many of those in the middle support an "alternative globalization." They accept globalization in general. However, they also want the international community to stop giving priority to the global market and trade. For many of the negative aspects of globalization to be addressed, the focus must shift to issues such as human and labor rights, the environment, and social welfare.

No matter how one may feel about the issue, globalization has influenced many aspects of everyday life for billions of people around the world. It is now more important than ever to understand the effects of globalization and to recognize its impact on the global community. ⌐

David Murphy protests Occidental Petroleum's drilling in Colombia.

People crossed the desert between Europe and Asia on the Silk Road.

THE ORIGINS
OF GLOBALIZATION

While the term *globalization* has been in use only for the past few decades, the concept is as old as human civilization.

More than 50,000 years ago, some of the very first humans left their homeland in East Africa and journeyed to other parts of the globe. Over time, humans spread across the continents and civilizations began to emerge. Through trade, curiosity, warfare, and conquest, people within these civilizations began interacting with one another. As a result, knowledge, culture, and groups of people spread to other regions.

Throughout history, trading foreign goods and learning the values and ideas of other cultures have played a role in influencing society. The Silk Road spanned two continents and connected major civilizations. China, India, Egypt, and Rome were able to trade goods with one another along this route. It is responsible for spreading Buddhism in East Asia. It also introduced gunpowder, printing, and the compass from Asia to Europe. The Silk Road also played a part in influencing religion, food, art, and other areas of culture.

The Silk Road

For thousands of years, the Silk Road served as a route connecting the East with the West. The Silk Road was not just one single road but a series of different routes connecting various settlements. These routes ranged as far east as China to as far west as Rome. Contrary to its name, silk was not the only product traded along this route. Precious metals, ivory, spices, and animals were carried over the long journey across two continents.

Goods on the Silk Road passed through a number of hands before arriving at their final destinations. People often acted as middlemen along the route, such as the Parthians, who bought silk from China and sold it in Rome. Romans bought silk more than most other goods brought along the route. However, the Romans were not the ones to name the route. The term *Silk Road* was coined by a nineteenth-century scholar in Germany named Baron Ferdinand von Richthofen.

Trading also sparked the desire for exploration. In 1492, Christopher Columbus embarked on a journey hoping to find a new route to East Asia. Instead, Columbus discovered the New World. The rediscovery of the Americas brought valuable crops such as the potato, the cocoa bean, and tobacco to Europe and Asia. It also brought new people and new forms of government to the Americas.

The Americas

One of globalization's many benefits is that it allows different cultures to interact with one another. But it also has many drawbacks. Trade and exploration sometimes lead to war and conquest of valuable land. Colonization of the Americas displaced millions of the original inhabitants and also encouraged the use of slave trade. Slaves were forced to work the newly conquered land. Also, colonists often carried diseases to the Americas that the American Indians had never faced. They were unable to fight off the diseases and in some areas, three out of every four American Indians were killed by these diseases.

THE INDUSTRIAL REVOLUTION

Beginning in the late eighteenth century, the Industrial Revolution spurred economic growth. Economies in Great Britain, France, and many other Western countries soared. The steam engine and railway system came into use. Electricity was harnessed. Improved financial structures and better mining techniques contributed to an increase in jobs and an improved standard of living.

Steel factories in England during the Industrial Revolution

Such advancements also caused many social changes within the Western nations. Large numbers of people moved from the countryside into the cities. Thousands of people who had once owned or worked on farms now worked in factories that produced massive amounts of goods. Commercial farming became more prevalent and supplied vast amounts of food for the swelling city populations. In addition, technological advancements allowed for faster and easier methods of communication and transportation.

Advances in Agriculture

During the eighteenth and nineteenth centuries, Great Britain experienced great agricultural growth. This growth was thanks to mechanically advanced farming techniques. The better farming techniques meant fewer people were needed to work the land. Thousands of people were then able to work in the factories, which helped fill factory jobs that were becoming more in demand because of mechanical improvements in factories as well.

As these industrializing countries experienced productivity and growth, trade between them grew exponentially. Trade with countries outside the industrializing realm grew as well. Many industrializing countries supported, at varying levels, the concept of free trade. Free trade between countries involves low or no trading barriers. High tariffs or government regulations are examples of trade barriers. Countries that supported free trade experienced growth, which gave them a political edge. Their dominance made them able to influence world policies and trade regulations.

By the nineteenth century, Great Britain had developed a leading economy with the emergence of the Industrial Revolution. In Europe, Britain and France had become very influential.

CONFLICTS, LOSS, AND GAIN

Great Britain, France, the United States, and many other Western countries prospered due to the advances during the Industrial Revolution. However, much of the rest of the world was not as fortunate. Many countries were still under colonial rule, dominated by Europe. Great Britain possessed colonies from the Americas to India to Australia. Although these colonial countries contributed to the Industrial Revolution by exporting resources, few—if any—received substantial benefits. Other countries, especially those under totalitarian regimes, remained closed off to free trade. These countries were unwilling to open their markets to foreigners.

With each passing decade, the rift between the industrializing countries and other nations was becoming more evident. Traditional ways of living were changing. But with those changes, new conflicts emerged.

The onset of World War I in 1914 caused international unease. At this time, many countries placed protectionist barriers on international trade. They required heavy tariffs, or taxes, on exported or imported goods. As a result, international trade slowed. Most economies were weakened by the war. By 1918, the war was over. Numerous countries were left with overturned governments and weak economies.

U.S. troops in France during World War I

While much of Europe struggled throughout the 1920s, the United States experienced an economic boom. The United States soon replaced Great Britain as the world's economic leader. But by the 1930s, the Great Depression had replaced the prosperity of the 1920s. Virtually all of North America and Western Europe were affected by the Depression. In this turbulent period, Hitler rose to power in Germany. By the end of the decade, economic and political unrest in Europe erupted in World War II. The Allies, made up mostly of democratic countries, eventually won the war. And the United States—suffering far less damage than most European countries—soon took on a dominant international role.

But the United States was not alone in its position. The Soviet Union, made up of Russia and several other Eastern European countries, assumed a powerful international influence as well. The Soviet Union endorsed communism. This is a system in which the production of goods is controlled by the government. This system was in contrast to that of the United States. The world soon faced the Cold War. The Soviet Union and the United States tried to exert their political influence over other countries. Neither the United States nor the Soviet Union fought one another directly during the Cold War. Instead, they engaged in proxy wars. Each country backed third parties in other, smaller wars. These

An Industrial Leader

Throughout the 1920s, the United States became an industrial leader within the world. Most governments in Europe were ravaged by World War I and in the process of rebuilding. During that time, many countries borrowed money from the United States. They also imported U.S. crops. This fueled the U.S. economy. Productivity soared throughout most of the 1920s.

Nearing the end of the decade, the United States experienced a series of economic problems that brought it—and much of Europe—into the Great Depression. The U.S. economy did not recover until World War II, when productivity and output increased.

The Cold War

From 1945 to 1989, the Soviet Union and the United States engaged in a battle over values. It was known as the Cold War. Each country believed their government was superior. And each country wanted to spread its form of government—communism from the Soviet Union and democracy from the United States—to countries worldwide.

The world was largely divided between East and West. In the East, many governments became communist, such as North Korea, Vietnam, and China. In the West, governments were mostly democratic, with the exception of Cuba and a few other Latin American countries.

wars included the Korean War, the Vietnam War, and the Soviet-Afghan War. The Soviet Union and the United States each wanted to spread their form of government. As countries adopted communism or democracy, it increased the power and influence of the Soviet Union or the United States.

Over time, the communist system of government began to crumble. By 1989, the Soviet Union had collapsed and the Cold War came to a close. By the end of the twentieth century, many countries had implemented democratic forms of government. Governments throughout the world started lowering trade barriers and opening their economies to international trade. Technology continued to improve. Global communication and transportation became faster and easier. The world was quickly changing. However, some countries enjoyed the benefits of this global economy more so than others. ⌐

U.S. President Ronald Reagan meets with Soviet leader
Mikhail Gorbachev in 1985, toward the end of the Cold War.

Protests against the World Trade Organization in Seattle

INTERNATIONAL
ORGANIZATIONS

T ens of thousands of people poured into
downtown Seattle, Washington, between
November 26 and December 6 of 1999. People came
from all across the United States and represented
hundreds of different groups. These groups ranged

from the American Civil Liberties Union (ACLU)
to the Raging Grannies. They all came for the same
reason—to protest a meeting held by the World
Trade Organization (WTO) in downtown Seattle.
These protesters were concerned that the WTO had
continued to support trade and corporate interests at
the expense of human rights. The protests ended in
violence. Still, they brought attention to the issues of
human rights, labor rights, and the environment as
they are impacted by globalization.

WORLD TRADE

The WTO is one organization of many
established since 1960 to oversee the world's
economic concerns. The world's economy became
more crucial with the spread of technology and trade
through globalization. The goal of organizations
such as the WTO has been to increase economic
security, decrease poverty, and aid countries in
economic crisis. These organizations have played a
fundamental role in the global economy. However,
not everyone agrees with just how much power these
organizations should have.

The WTO is paired with sister organizations—the
World Bank and the International Monetary Fund

(IMF). These organizations began with the Bretton Woods agreement. Several industrialized countries formed this agreement in 1944. At the end of World War II, the leaders of the Allied nations came together to establish a stable and liberal international economic system. From that, the IMF, the General Agreement on Tariffs and Trade (GATT) treaty, and the World Bank were formed.

The Bretton Woods agreement was formed during a critical era. The Allied nations were on the verge of winning World War II. World War I and the economic crises of the 1930s were not a distant memory. The Allied nations wanted to avoid repeating those difficult times. Those participating in the Bretton Woods agreement mostly came from

Protest in Seattle

Throughout the WTO protest week in Seattle, more than 700 different groups participated in the demonstrations. The groups represented a number of interests, from the environment to education. Some of the groups that participated in the WTO protest included:

- Animal Welfare Institute
- Canadian Labour Congress
- Chilean Ecological Action Network
- Greenpeace
- Indigenous Environmental Network
- National Farmers Union
- Raging Grannies
- Rainforest Action Network
- Sea Turtle Restoration Project
- Washington Association for Churches
- World Forum of Fish Harvesters and Fishworkers

democratic countries. Many favored capitalist
markets in which businesses and goods were privately
owned. The planners wanted to create an open
international market in which trade barriers and
tariffs were limited. They believed the open market
would help all countries involved. Their goal was
to improve the standard of living across the world,
decreasing chances for war.

U.S. Secretary of State Cordell Hull, one
such planner, said that with freer trade and stable
economic systems,

> *. . . one country would not be deadly jealous of another and
> the living standards of all countries might rise, thereby
> eliminating the economic dissatisfaction that breeds war.*[1]

Since the Bretton Woods negotiations, it has
been disputed whether these organizations benefit or
worsen the global community.

THE INTERNATIONAL MONETARY FUND AND WORLD BANK

The IMF was ratified on December 27, 1945,
when the first 29 countries signed the Articles of
Agreement. As of 2008, 185 countries belong to
the IMF. Those countries all contribute to a "pool,"

The World Bank is located in Washington DC.

from which member countries experiencing crises may borrow money to stabilize their economies.

The IMF also makes plans and policies for countries experiencing economic hardships. A new plan is designed for each situation to help with specific problems. These include debt, natural disasters, high unemployment, or improper exchange rates.

The IMF often works with the World Bank. The World Bank was established to provide loans and grants to countries and to advise on economic decisions. Both the World Bank and the IMF have developed many debt relief policies. The IMF and World Bank also provide support services for countries in deep poverty.

While these policies appear to be beneficial, the IMF and the World Bank are not always effective. This is often seen in their work with the developing world. One of the key arguments concerning the IMF and the World Bank is trade liberalization. Trade liberalization removes or loosens restrictions on trade. Typically, a country has trade barriers to protect its industries. If trade barriers are lifted, products from foreign markets may enter the country. Oftentimes, these products are priced at cheaper rates than domestic products. If fewer domestic products are being sold, a country could risk high unemployment and decreased wealth.

These institutions also have been accused of advising developing

NGOs

As the world becomes more connected, nongovernmental organizations, or NGOs, are gaining influence. Generally, NGOs are nonprofit organizations. NGOs are private organizations that work to promote social causes. Human rights groups, environmental organizations, and animal welfare associations are all examples of NGOs. Some NGOs have only a small number of members. Others are large organizations, such as Greenpeace or Amnesty International. These NGOs are influencing international decisions that once were only handled by governments. Whether or not NGOs are beneficial is disputed. But many people agree that these groups will only gain in number and influence.

countries to open up their trade barriers too soon. This may cause the country's economy to destabilize—something the IMF and World Bank are meant to prevent. Joseph E. Stiglitz, author of *Globalization and Its Discontents*, argues,

> . . . most of the advanced industrial countries—including the United States and Japan—had built up their economies by wisely and selectively protecting some of their industries until they were strong enough to compete with foreign companies. . . . Forcing a developing country to open itself up to imported products that would compete with those produced by certain of its industries, . . . can have disastrous consequences—socially and economically. [2]

In the past, the IMF and World Bank have implemented policies of increasing taxes on a country's citizens. These taxes are intended to decrease government debt. However, they also increase poverty within the country.

Many countries also make cutbacks in social services and government subsidies on the advice of the IMF and World Bank. Citizens face hardships due to these cutbacks. Subsidies help offset the price of certain goods and services. When subsidies are cut, the price of those goods increases. Health care, child care, and education are other things that can get cut. Though cutbacks save the government money, the citizens are the ones who lose.

The World Trade Organization

When the GATT agreement was placed into force in 1948, its primary objective was to reduce trade barriers. One way the GATT agreement tries to achieve this is by lowering tariffs. It also settles trade disputes between countries. When the WTO was established in 1995, it took on the responsibilities of the GATT.

The WTO states it is an organization that benefits the global community by providing a forum for countries to settle trade disputes. Since it was founded, the WTO has handled more than 300 disputes between member countries. A number of those disputes could have turned into larger conflicts—such as war—had the WTO not mediated. The WTO also reduces trade inequities between countries. Every decision is made by the agreement of

Service Industry Expansion

In 1995, the WTO produced the General Agreement on Trade in Services (GATS) treaty. This treaty allows the service industry to expand internationally. The service industry includes private companies that provide health, education, or utility services. Many social services are operated by a country's government. But with the GATS treaty, international corporations are now able to privatize certain service industries, such as educational services and water utilities.

all participating member countries. It is possible that without the WTO, larger countries would be able to more freely impose their own trade requirements on less-powerful trading partners.

However, the WTO is often seen as favoring international trade and corporate interest. This may be at the expense of human and labor rights, the environment, and animal protection. Janet Thomas, author of *The Battle in Seattle*, writes,

> The WTO's Article III . . . makes it unlawful for a government to discriminate against products that are . . . produced in ways that are destructive to people and/or the environment.[3]

Though the WTO attracts a fair share of criticism, many feel it is a necessary organization. The WTO is important in settling disputes and aiding struggling countries. However, many critics feel the WTO needs to change its focus. Instead of focusing solely on the economic issues, many believe it needs to look at the social impact of its policies.

Seattle protests against the World Trade Organization
gained national attention.

China's economic success has helped bring supermarkets to once-impoverished areas.

THE DEVELOPING WORLD

ntil the early twenty-first century, China was isolated and closed off to free trade. Its government controlled every aspect of the economy—and the lives of its citizens. For most people in China, life was difficult and many struggled just to get by. As of 2008, however, many urban Chinese citizens had become more affluent, owning refrigerators, washing machines, and televisions. Rural farmers were eating 48 percent more meat and more than 400 percent more fruit than they did a year before. The Chinese economy was soaring. Its influence was felt in most every region of the world. Wu Ying, editor in chief of the Chinese edition of *Elle* magazine, describes how much of the country has changed in only the past few years:

> *Maybe young women today don't know what it was like. But ten years ago I wouldn't have imagined myself wearing this blouse. When people bought clothes, they thought, "How long will this last?" A housewife knew that most of the monthly salary would be spent on food, and now it's just a small part, so she can think about what to wear or where to travel. And now with refrigerators, we don't have to buy food every day.* [1]

China's transformation from a struggling, developing nation into an economic giant—while not unique—is uncommon. Many developing nations are desperately trying to catch up with the industrialized world. And as the world becomes more globalized, the need for developing countries to enter the international community is more crucial. Globalization may help developing countries improve their standard of living and economies. But it also has the potential to do harm.

Growth Report

According to an IMF report, the developing world's portion in international trade increased from 19 percent in 1971 to 29 percent by 1999. China and other developing Asian countries experienced the most growth. This growth was due mostly to exporting manufactured products. Countries that exported mostly raw materials and agricultural products, such as many in Africa, experienced little or no increase in their share of global trade.

THE EFFECTS OF GLOBALIZATION ON DEVELOPING COUNTRIES

Over the past several decades, almost every developing country has received monetary aid. The aid has been provided through loans and grants from the International Monetary Fund (IMF), the World Bank, developed countries, and other organizations. The aid is to help promote industrialization.

Sometimes the aid given to developing countries does not promote growth. Since 1980, the United States has given $144 billion to 97 developing countries. Researchers looked at data from each country to measure its

Bolivian President Evo Morales and Brazilian President Luiz Inácio da Silva have agreed to work toward agricultural improvement in Bolivia.

economic growth. They found that over the 20-year period, only four of the ninety-seven countries experienced economic growth more than 1 percent. Twelve countries experienced economic decline.

Economists Richard Roll and John Talbott researched developing countries. They found that governments that promote civil and political liberties, free trade, and private business development experienced relatively fast economic growth. The rate of growth was much faster than countries with weak government structures, excessive

Doha Development Round

Over the last several years, many developing nations worked hard to lower trade barriers and abolish protectionist policies set up by industrialized countries. In November of 2001, the Doha Development Round began. It was overseen by the WTO. Developing nations were represented mainly by China, Brazil, India, and South Africa. The nations came together to negotiate with developed countries, led by the EU, the United States, and Japan. The negotiations continue but without reaching many compromises. However, the developing world's voice is becoming stronger. Developing countries may one day achieve trade agreements that benefit them.

regulations, and trade barriers. In a developing country with a strong government, assistance could be used well. It could help a country become more globalized and successful.

During the 1980s and 1990s, several Latin American countries suffered crises after first opening their markets to international trade. Many of these countries reformed their economic policies and fought governmental corruption. Many of their economies began to improve.

Today, in a survey of Latin Americans by the Pew Global Attitudes Project, the majority believes people are better off in open-market economies rather than closed markets. Despite hardships, many people continue to support a global economy. While there may be struggles along the way, developing countries can achieve lasting growth.

When opening their markets to free trade, many developing countries allow, or encourage, multinational corporations to operate within their borders. However, international corporations often benefit much more than developing countries. And the governments of many developing countries often favor corporations over the interests of citizens or the environment. For example, large agricultural corporations have taken over much of the land in developing countries. In South America, rain forests have been

Globalization in Ghana

In Africa, Ghana is a prime example of the good and bad effects of globalization. Ghana's economy grows by six percent every year. It has been able to keep inflation low and has paid nearly two-thirds of its debt. It also has a strong government and a growing middle class. However, China, another industrializing country, is mass-producing cheap goods and making it difficult for Ghana's products to compete internationally.

Nora Bannerman of Ghana is a fashion designer who owns Sleek Garments Export, a factory that makes handwoven traditional African cloth. Bannerman is struggling to sell her cloth overseas. China has started to mass-produce African cloth at a lower cost. Yet Bannerman cannot cut costs to make her cloth. She is required to pay her workers a certain wage under the U.S. African Growth and Opportunity Act. She is unable to save money by paying her employees less. Bannerman also struggles with high taxes on the imported thread she buys to produce her fabric. China has different trade agreements and working standards. China is able to produce the cloth at a much lower cost. This makes it much more difficult for workers in Ghana to compete.

destroyed to make way for farming and cattle ranching. Many of these countries are forced to rely on imported food products, as they are no longer able to grow their own crops.

Sometimes, developing countries are encouraged to open up their markets too soon. They open their markets before "safety nets," such as minimum wage and working condition standards, are put in place. Industrialized nations are then able to exploit these countries. They force developing countries to lower trade barriers while still keeping up many of their own. For example, the European Union (EU) protects its farmers from competition with other countries—particularly those in the developing world. The EU's Common Agriculture Policy (CAP) places high quotas and tariffs on agricultural imports from other

Optimistic Outlook

A 2007 survey by the Pew Global Attitudes Project found that in nine out of ten African countries, most people believed that their standard of living would improve in five years. The survey also found that the majority of people living in Kenya, Tanzania, and Uganda had gone without food within the past year because they could not afford it.

countries. These measures block countries from importing their food into the EU. According to the UN Conference on Trade Development, if the EU did not use the CAP, developing countries could make an estimated $700 billion in food exports to Europe each year. This amount is nearly 14 times more than what the developing world receives in international aid. In addition, excess food from the EU is dumped on developing countries as food subsidies. This further hurts farmers in the developing world. They are unable to sell their own products— even within their own countries. The United States and other developed countries have similar policies that hurt the developing world.

Millennium Development Goals

At its Millennium Summit in 2000, the United Nations (UN) agreed upon a set of Millennium

"There is just one road, and it's the road, I believe, of free markets, of liberalized markets, and liberalized politics. . . . Every country should go down the road in a way that is consistent with maintaining its cultural cohesion, its social cohesion, but at the same time its economic development. For some it might be 5 miles an hour, for others it may be 50. But promise me you just won't do one thing—not go down the road at all. If you do that, I promise you, you'll bring nothing but ruin and devastation to your people."[2]
—Thomas L. Friedman,
New York Times
foreign affairs columnist

Development Goals that it planned to reach by 2015. The issues included: hunger, poverty, universal primary education, gender equality, child health, maternal health, combating HIV/AIDS and malaria, environmental stability, and global partnership for development.

The goals attend to both social and economic issues faced by developing nations. The UN goals seek to open trade barriers faced by developing nations and aid in debt relief. However, these goals are also socially responsible and take into account the poverty and poor health that citizens face.

A worker on a pineapple plantation in San Ignacio, Nicaragua,
where tariffs will be lifted to aid free trade

Outsourcing has created jobs in Dakar, Senegal.

THE DEVELOPED WORLD

ccording to the World Trade
Organization (WTO), one of the
benefits of globalization is that free trade cuts
the cost of living. It also provides consumers with
inexpensive goods. But some people in the developed

world are questioning if inexpensive products are worth the drawbacks. Such drawbacks include losing jobs to overseas locations and fueling a growing anti-Western sentiment.

One of the primary concerns about globalization in the developed world is centered on the issue of outsourcing. This occurs when a company buys international goods or services at a lower cost than those that could be obtained locally.

OUTSOURCING AND DEVELOPED COUNTRIES

In order to save money and increase products, many companies from developed nations outsource jobs to developing countries. Many of those in the developing world are helped by outsourcing. It provides them with jobs and fuels their nation's economy. Their countries become wealthier. This increases the developing nation's spending power. The demand increases for more services and goods from the developed countries that originally

"Two basic changes are happening today under the impact of globalization. In western countries, not only public institutions but also everyday life are becoming opened up from the hold of tradition. And other societies across the world that remained more traditional are becoming [detraditionalized]. . . . This is a society living after the end of nature. Few aspects of the physical world, in other words, are any longer just natural—unaffected by human intervention."[1]
—*Anthony Giddens,*
Runaway World

Skilled and Unskilled Jobs

A recent U.S. Bureau of Labor and Statistics report listed the fastest-growing occupations in the United States. Network systems and data communications specialists, and personal and home care aides topped the list. More than half of these jobs required an associate's degree or higher. According to a study done by the University of California-Berkeley, an estimated 14 million Americans could lose their jobs to outsourcing over the next few years. Many of those are jobs that require a high level of skill.

outsourced jobs. In the developed countries, any jobs lost to outsourcing could be replaced with higher skilled jobs, particularly within the service industry. As long as developed countries provide educational resources for displaced workers, they can gain skills to find different jobs. The economies then will continue to prosper.

However, many workers who have lost their jobs to outsourcing are not able to find new jobs. It is not just workers in manual labor who struggle. Jobs involving a high level of skill are moving to developing nations as well. As labor moves to developing areas, industrialized nations may face rising unemployment and falling economies. One study by Forrester Research estimates that more than 3.5 million jobs will move to developing areas by 2015. Most of these jobs will require college educations or a high level of skill.

Gallup polled Americans on outsourcing during the 2000s. The poll found that 61 percent of

Americans expressed concern that they or someone they know could lose their job to outsourcing. Those in the field of electrical engineering especially have reason to fear. Their unemployment rate in the United States is at 6.2 percent. That figure is above the national average. Electrical engineers are losing their jobs to overseas candidates. These new workers are paid at a much lower rate.

PROTECTIONISM

Globalization has often been seen as a reason for outsourcing and loss of jobs in industrialized countries. It can also fuel anti-Western sentiment from the developing world. Author of *In Defense*

Agriculture

Industrialized nations spend an estimated $350 billion per year supporting farming in their own countries through protectionist policies and trade barriers. These policies encourage local farm development and make agricultural imports more costly. These nations benefit from such policies because it encourages agricultural growth and ensures that local farmers will be able to sell their products. However, such policies have a negative impact on developing nations, which struggle to find a market for their own agricultural products.

When industrialized nations have a farming surplus, this, too, has a negative impact on developing nations. Surpluses are often dumped on developing nations as subsidies. These subsidies can be sold at lower costs than locally farmed produce. When this happens, local farmers cannot find a market for their produce even within their own countries.

When industrialized nations get rid of their surplus in this way, they do not do so with the intention of harming developing nations. They are simply trying to do what is best for the people in their own countries.

of Global Capitalism, Johan Norberg states,

> We in the West used to tell the developing countries about
> the benefits of the free market. And we promised wealth and
> progress would certainly come if they changed and adopted
> our ways. . . . No wonder, then, that Western countries are
> seen as hypocrites, producing resentment and a fertile ground
> for anti-American and anti-liberal ideas in many regions at
> a time when the West needs friends more than ever.[2]

Indeed, the WTO estimated that European
protectionism of agriculture costs an average family
in the EU $1,500 (USD) more per year for the price
of food. Trade barriers on clothing have also cost
industrialized countries.

However, many hope to eliminate such policies
and trade barriers. If trade barriers were eliminated,
it could save consumers money in developed
countries. It could possibly reduce anti-Westernism
in developing nations. The standard of living could
increase in countries participating in free trade.
In turn, this would promote peace. But whether
free trade would promote international stability
is a complex and controversial issue. It continues
to be disputed among governments and citizens
throughout the world.

The EU's CAP helps shape Britain's farming industry.

Senegalese illegal immigrants expelled from the Canary Islands

MIGRATION

hot African sun beats down on the thousands of unemployed, uneducated youths of Dakar, Senegal. Many stare longingly out across the Atlantic Ocean. Hundreds of miles away lie the Canary Islands and the gateway to Spain and then onward to Europe. Many Senegalese feel Spain offers the hope to achieve a better life. In 2006, about 15,000 Senegalese risked their lives by traveling hundreds of miles across the ocean. Many traveled in makeshift boats to reach the Canary Islands. But they are not the only ones. Each year, millions of people all over the world attempt to cross borders in the hopes of achieving a successful life in a foreign land.

Migration, or the movement of people, has always been a part of human history. It is a cornerstone of globalization. Since the very first humans migrated from Africa thousands of years ago, migration has been intertwined with globalization. Through migration, cultures have become more connected. Migration has helped make the world's regions more dependent on one another.

REASONS FOR MIGRATION

Several factors lead people to leave their homelands for new and foreign places. Often, people do not want to leave their native countries but are forced to do so to find better

Poverty

Many immigrants leave their own countries due to poverty. Immigration may not always help them achieve a much higher standard of living. A recent study of U.S. immigrants found that 17 percent live in poverty. By comparison, only 9 percent of U.S. citizens live in poverty.

lives. When a country has high unemployment and poverty rates, many people often choose to take a chance elsewhere. They go to where jobs offer better earnings.

War and persecution are two other factors that compel people to leave their countries. Migrants may flee the conflict in their homeland for the safety and refuge found in another country. Sometimes, these refugees are granted asylum in the host country. A host country provides a legal, safe haven for displaced people. During the 1950s, the Chinese government took over Tibet, a country to its west. In so doing, it brutally suppressed any who opposed the military invasion. Thousands of Tibetan refugees fled to the neighboring countries of Nepal and India. Other times, migrants fleeing persecution overwhelm the host countries. For example, Jordan has seen an influx of migrants from Iraq. However, Jordan's economy has become strained by such an increase in its population.

Natural disasters, such as earthquakes, floods, fires, and hurricanes may cause people to migrate to other areas. Such disasters often have damaging effects on the area. People who survive a disaster often lose their homes, possessions, jobs, and sense of belonging. These people are often forced to move to other areas as a means to survive.

People have migrated since early human history. One of the largest waves of migration coincided with the Industrial Revolution. Many consider this period to be the first era of modern globalization. Ten percent of the world's population immigrated to other countries from the 1850s to the 1900s. Advancements in technology and transportation contributed to this increase. However, by the 1930s countries worldwide started feeling the effects of economic depressions. They also experienced the conflicts of World War I and World War II.

Migration declined drastically. By the later half of the century, worldwide migration was once again increasing.

From 1990 to 2005, about 36 million people migrated to other countries. Many of these immigrants did so illegally. Of those 36 million immigrants, 33 million chose to immigrate to

> "Globalization—the growing interconnectedness and increasingly tighter interdependence among people of the planet—is a historical process that began at the dawn of time, when our ancestors stepped out of East Africa. . . . The adventurers and migrants—who have since the dawn of history been the principal actors of globalization—are now seen as major threats to the stability of a globalized world. Immigration laws have been tightening against a rising tide of poor migrants, estimated at 200 million in 2005."[1]
> —Nayan Chanda, PhD Director of Publications and the editor of Yale Global Online

1882 Chinese Exclusion Act

The Chinese Exclusion Act of 1882 was the first piece of legislation in the United States that prohibited immigrants from legally entering the country for a period of ten years. Enacted on May 6, 1882, the act was intended to keep Chinese laborers out of the country. Many people were prejudiced against the Chinese and other minorities. The act sought to limit Chinese influence in the country.

industrialized nations. Most of those came from areas of severe poverty, conflict, or other hardships. Victor Hanson, a senior fellow at the Hoover Institution, describes the reasoning behind this mass exodus to industrialized nations:

> *Thousands of aliens crossing our 2,000-mile border from an impoverished Mexico reflect a much larger global one-way traffic problem. In Germany, Turkish workers—both legal and illegal—are desperate to find either permanent residence or citizenship. . . . Albanians flock to Greece to do farm work, and then are regularly deported for doing so illegally. . . . Stable democracies and free markets ensure economic growth, rising standards of living and, thus, lots of jobs, while these countries' birth rates and native populations fall. In contrast, immigrants usually flee mostly failed states that cannot offer their people any real hope of prosperity and security.* [2]

Undoubtedly, millions of these immigrants choose to migrate to the industrialized world from developing countries in order to escape the hardships of their own countries. The difference between the developed nations and those that are developing is profound. Most of the developed nations offer strong economies. There are possibilities for work and higher earnings, plus better education, health, and overall living standards.

BENEFITS AND PITFALLS

Immigrants generally choose to leave their original countries for an opportunity to improve their

NAFTA and Immigration

Many people feel that the impact globalization has on free trade has had a significant effect on immigration. There is concern about illegal immigration to developed countries.

The North American Free Trade Agreement (NAFTA) is one example that some use to describe globalization's impact on the immigration debate. NAFTA called for North American countries to lower trade barriers among one another. These countries were to allow for a free flow of goods across borders. Critics contend that once NAFTA was implemented, it wiped out many small Mexican farms. Inexpensive agricultural products made their way from the United States across the Mexican border. Mexican farmers could no longer keep up with such cheap products from the United States. Few Mexican citizens were willing to pay more for food grown on Mexican soil.

Before NAFTA, the rate of illegal immigration from Mexico to the United States had decreased by 18 percent. Then, cheaper agricultural products from the United States flooded the Mexican market. An estimated 2 million farming families were driven out of business. Many of those farmers chose to emigrate to the United States. In the first eight years after NAFTA was imposed, illegal immigration from Mexico to the United States increased by more than 61 percent.

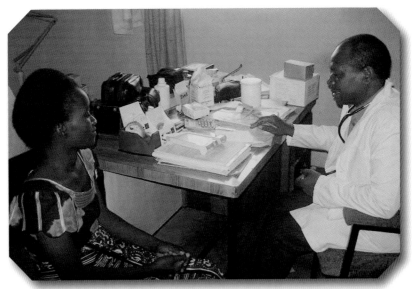

Malawi needs more doctors working within its borders.

quality of life. The countries that immigrants
migrate to often stand to benefit as well.
Immigration to developed countries can help fill
labor shortages. This also boosts the overall economy
with more people in the workforce.

The developing countries that lose people to
emigration also stand to benefit. Often, family
members who remain behind receive remittances. A
remittance is money that is sent home to the family
by those working abroad. This money can have a
profound effect on a developing country's economy.

In the small country of Somalia, it is estimated that $200 million to $500 million a year is sent home from abroad. That amount is four times more than what Somalia's main export brings in. And humanitarian aid in the country amounts to only $60 million.

Yet many people in industrialized nations are becoming increasingly wary of the high rates of immigration to their countries. In European and North American nations, as well as other industrialized countries, some governments and citizens are experiencing an anti-immigration sentiment. Some people feel that immigrants lower wages and put an added strain on the welfare system.

Developing countries may also be hurt when their skilled workers emigrate elsewhere. Social scientists cite what is often called "brain drain." Developing countries often lose their trained and educated citizens to countries that offer better wages or higher standards of living. For example, the African nation of Malawi is experiencing a shortage in medical personnel. Malawi has only 10 percent of the doctors it needs. Fourteen percent of the population in Malawi lives with HIV/AIDS. It is estimated that there are more Malawian doctors practicing

Attitudes toward Illegal Immigration

A recent survey of Americans' attitudes toward illegal immigration revealed mixed feelings:
• Sixty-six percent felt illegal immigrants take jobs that U.S. citizens would normally not fill.
• Sixty-four percent believed illegal immigrants should be able to obtain some level of legal status in the United States.

medicine in Manchester, England, than in all of Malawi—a country with a population of 13 million people.

The movement of people has always been a part of human history. Increased transportation, communication, and a widening gap between developed and developing countries will continue to persuade people to migrate. Migration, just like the free flow of goods and ideas across borders, is an important part of globalization. ⌐

Somalia receives more money in remittances than it does from exports.

U.S. trade representative Robert Portman speaks on improving world stability through free trade.

INTERNATIONAL STABILITY

The collapse of the Soviet Union in 1989 ended the long struggle between communism and democracy. Freedom House, a U.S. organization that tracks democracy throughout the world, conducted a survey in 1999–2000. Of the

192 countries surveyed, 85 were considered "free," while another 59 were classified as "partly free." In a follow-up survey in 2002–2003, Freedom House determined that 63 percent of the world's governments are now democratically elected. That is a 23-percent increase in democratic governments throughout the world since the mid-1980s.

Globalization has contributed to the increase in democracy. Internet, satellite television, and other media have aided global communication and the spread of ideas. Free trade has also opened up many once-closed markets, allowing prodemocracy influences to affect societies.

DEMOCRACY

Oftentimes, international trade brought on by globalization is seen as a key factor in bringing democracy to a country. Economist Milton Friedman took this view in his book, *Capitalism and Freedom*:

> The kind of economic organization that provides economic freedom . . . also promotes political freedom because it separates economic power from political power and in this way enables the one to offset the other.[1]

Economists James Gwartney and Robert Lawson found that from 1980 to 1998, countries that were most open to free trade experienced more economic growth than nations that were the most closed off to free trade.

That growth generally spurred a higher standard of living among a country's citizens and a growing middle class. Free trade through globalization creates a larger middle class. This middle class is better able to influence the political structure. Governments will often provide for more civil liberties and rights—leading to a more democratic society.

Globalization and the Cold War

The collapse of the Soviet Union was a crucial turning point in history. For decades, the East and the West had been fighting an ideological war, called the Cold War. The battle was between democracy and communism, with each attempting to eradicate the other.

While the communist Soviet Union had a very strong military, space program, and economy at certain points, it failed to last. As globalization spread throughout the world, the closed-off market in the Soviet Union suffered. Finally, the Soviet Union dissolved when it became undeniable that the regime could no longer prosper.

In 1991, Boris Yeltsin, leader of the USSR, declared:

Our country has not been lucky. Indeed, it was decided to carry out this Marxist [communist] experiment on us—fate pushed us precisely in this direction. In the end we proved that there's no place for this idea. It has simply pushed us off the path the world's civilized countries have taken.[2]

Still, not everyone is convinced. Sometimes free trade and globalization do not lead to democracy. When a nondemocratic government opens the market to free trade, citizens may attribute any benefits coming from the open market to their governments. If most people see these advances as being caused by the government, they will not support reform. For example, China has seen an increase in economic growth and living standard over the last five years. Because of this growth, 89 percent of Chinese citizens view the government favorably.

In addition, countries such as Argentina, Kenya, Thailand, and Russia have all experienced problems that have led to economic recessions and other crises when transitioning to democratic governments and open-market economies. While these economic troubles have a variety of

Free Trade, Open Markets, and Democracy

While free trade, open markets, and democracy often go hand in hand, not all countries experience them equally. Singapore has one of the world's largest and most successful open-market economies. Yet it is not a fully democratic state. In contrast, India has a stable and thriving democracy. Until recent years, however, its market remained mostly closed off to international trade.

causes, many have become resentful of industrial and democratic institutions.

War and Terrorism

Both free trade and democracy have increased globally since the 1960s. However, the disarmament of weapons across nations is still an issue. Globalization's impact on conflict—both national and international—has been mixed. Globalization has furthered peace through nuclear weapons treaties and peace negotiations. However, in some areas it has had negative effects on establishing peace. Increased terrorism, civil wars, and ethnic and religious violence are all major causes for concern.

In general, countries that participate in trade with one another are less likely to engage in war. Trade between Western European countries has given the

"[Globalization] is the reason for the revival of local cultural identities in different parts of the world. If one asks, for example, why the Scots want more independence in the UK, or why there is a strong separatist movement in Quebec, the answer is not to be found only in their cultural history. Local nationalisms spring up as a response to [globalizing] tendencies, as the hold of older nation-states weakens."[3]

—*Anthony Giddens, Runaway World*

continent an unprecedented 60 years of peace. And although enemy countries such as India and Pakistan both possess nuclear weapons, they are less likely to engage in warfare due to the negative effects it would have on their economies.

The World Trade Organization (WTO) is an advocate of free trade. The WTO promotes free trade for its effects on global stability. As stated on its Web site,

> . . . smoothly-flowing trade also helps people all over the world become better off. People who are more prosperous and contented are also less likely to fight.[4]

However, the effects of free trade have also led to instability and violence. Free trade is intended to generate wealth in a country and help its citizens. Yet sometimes wealth generated by free trade only helps foreign investors, corporations, or those in the upper class. This can fuel anger and resentment in those still living in poor conditions. The people may lash out in the form of civil

"We now know that order grows out of chaos. You cannot have significant change, especially on the scale of Russia or China, without conflict. Not conflicts between East and West, or North and South, but 'wave' conflicts between industrially dominant countries and predominantly agrarian countries, or conflicts within countries making a transition from one to the other."[5]
—*Erla Zwingle*

war, or terrorism. Steven Staples, chairman of the International Network on Disarmament and Globalization, writes,

Universal Expansion

Some fear that corporations may soon be overtaking outer space. U.S. Space Command has created a space program, In Vision for 2020. This program already claims it is "dominating the space dimension of military operations to protect U.S. interests and investments."[7]

> *There are more wars being fought today—mostly in the Third World—than there were during the Cold War. Most are not wars between countries, but are civil wars. . . . Financial instability, economic inequality, competition for resources, and environmental degradation—all root causes of war—are exacerbated by globalization.*[6]

As major corporations spread across the globe, the military interests that protect them spread too. Industrial countries often build up their military to protect their nation's corporate interests overseas. The United States, for instance, has greatly increased its military capacity since the Cold War.

Globalization's effects on world stability, democracy, and peace remain controversial. Other closely related controversial issues include globalization's effects on human rights and poverty.

UN Secretary General Kofi Annan speaks on global disarmament.

UN Commission on Human Rights meets
in Geneva, Switzerland, in 2006.

HUMAN RIGHTS

In December 1948, only three years after
World War II had ended, members of
the United Nations (UN) General Assembly came
together to draft the Universal Declaration of
Human Rights. It included 30 articles, or rules.

These articles outlined, among other things, the rights to an education, equality, and employment regardless of country or territory. Some of the most basic rights were the rights to "a standard of living adequate for the health and well-being" of a person, and the right to ensure "an existence worthy of human dignity."[1]

More than half a century later, globalization's influence on the world has led to drastic changes in the way many people live. Yet the most basic human rights remain just as essential. As globalization's effects spread across the world, many question if globalization will help or hurt the progress of human rights.

HUMAN RIGHTS

Globalization has often been viewed as a driving force behind the spread of human rights. Oftentimes, countries in which human rights are readily applied influence other nations that do not enforce human rights laws. Pressure from the global community can force countries to

Human Rights Report

The 2007 Human Rights Report, released by the U.S. Department of State, found that countries with the worst human rights records were mostly countries following totalitarian regimes. The report listed Belarus, Burma, China, Cuba, the Democratic People's Republic of Korea, Iran, Uzbekistan, and Zimbabwe as some of the countries with the worst human rights records. The report also listed countries that have seen notable improvements in human rights. These included the Balkans, Colombia, and Uganda.

conform at the risk of losing international support. Many nations rely on such support through loans, investment, and tourism.

As more countries open up their markets and democratize their governments, human rights will also advance. Ukraine is one such example. The people of this nation have democratically elected a new government. Since then, there has been more accountability for human rights violations. Ukraine's human rights performance has risen considerably. In addition, international groups such as the UN and Human Rights Watch have documented countries' failures to uphold human rights. These organizations have put pressure on such countries to become more accountable.

Still, international pressure for human rights is not always effective. For example, there has been international pressure on Saudi Arabia to end laws that limit women's rights. One such law in Saudi Arabia punishes a woman for being raped. Despite international

Women's Rights in Saudi Arabia

Saudi Arabia has often been accused of human rights violations. In particular, Saudi Arabia has a poor track record regarding women's rights. Women are not allowed to ride bicycles or to drive. They are also not allowed to leave their homes without being escorted by a male relative. Adult women are required to wear a head-to-toe black cloak, called an *abaaya*. About 70 percent of university students are women; however, they make up only 5 percent of the workforce.

Laborers in Hong Kong demand improved workers' rights.

pressure, Saudi Arabia continues to enforce laws that violate women's rights.

However, opening up a country's market does not guarantee human rights advancement. China, for example, has a large stake in international trade. Yet the country continues to restrict its citizens and violate human rights.

WORKERS' RIGHTS

As globalization continues to take its hold, a continuing flood of corporations have moved overseas for cheaper labor and less restrictive environmental regulations. Many of these companies operate sweatshops. Workers are forced to withstand poor working conditions and minimal pay.

It can also be argued that a number of international companies should uphold the same regulations and labor rights for their overseas employees as they would for their domestic workers. This could provide overseas workers better working conditions and fairer labor standards than they would have otherwise.

The issues surrounding human rights often are part of the issue of poverty. People living in poverty often lack the most basic rights. Food, shelter, access to health care, and

---

Sweatshops

Many international corporations offer fair wages and decent working conditions to their employees. However, some organizations operate "sweatshop factories." Workers are required to work long hours with little pay. In a garment factory in El Salvador, female workers were only allowed two bathroom breaks a day. Women at the factory were required to take pregnancy tests. If they were found to be pregnant, they were fired. Workers were also forced to work overtime and would be fired for refusing.

The women made only 60 cents an hour—earning about one-third the cost of living. The women were also required to pay for the pregnancy tests. They paid $1.63 a day for day care if they needed it. The WTO felt the wage was too high and recommended that it be lowered to 36 cents an hour.

Charlie Kernaghan, executive director of the National Labor Committee says, "Women in El Salvador are raising their children on coffee, because they can't afford milk."[2]

clean drinking water are difficult to come by. In addition, people in poverty may not be able to obtain an education. Those in poverty often struggle simply to stay alive. Globalization's impact on poverty has had mixed results. The poverty rate has dropped in most regions. But more than a third of the global population still lives without access to electricity or clean drinking water.

Better Jobs

Rajan Bakshi, a lawyer in New Delhi, India, believes that multinational corporations provide better jobs than the local industry. "I think the average worker is better off with the multinationals. I see these young people at the satellite companies—girls who are 24, 25. If they'd been working in an Indian company, they'd have been exploited. Smart young people now have options because of multinationals."[3]

POVERTY

International trade generally increases wealth. But it does not always distribute that wealth equally. The International Monetary Fund (IMF) reported that the gap between rich and poor countries has grown within the past several decades. The gap between people within countries has grown as well.

Economist Xavier Sala-i-Martin found that global income inequality has decreased since 1980. While poverty may always be an issue, many organizations are taking steps to reduce poverty. These organizations provide loans and other resources to countries in need.

The IMF insists that the standard of living in many of today's poor countries is better than the standard of living experienced by even the richest of countries a century earlier.

However, at times, the IMF and World Bank have implemented programs in countries that have worsened the effects of poverty. The IMF has advocated programs that have increased taxes on the poor in order to help a government pay off its debts. One-time project director of the International Forum on Globalization, Antonia Juhasz, states,

> *The policies of economic globalization . . . concentrate wealth at the top, removing from governments and communities the very tools needed to ensure equity and to protect workers, social services, the environment, and sustainable livelihoods. In this way, economic globalization and its institutions— including the International Monetary Fund (IMF), the World Bank, the World Trade Organization . . . have created the most dramatic increase in global inequality . . . and have increased global poverty.* [4]

Globalization and the organizations that surround it can have a crucial impact on the world. Nowhere is this impact more crucial than on world health and the environment.

*Many children in Mozambique are malnourished
due to widespread poverty.*

The Sasol fuel refinement plant, a World Bank development program, may be at risk because of climate change.

HEALTH AND THE ENVIRONMENT

cross the United States, much of the available food has traveled an estimated 1,500 miles (2,400 km) before arriving at the local supermarket. Foreign markets and the advances made in transportation have made food exports a good option for many countries. It also has had major effects on the environment and world health.

The Environment

As countries open their markets to compete with other economies, the quality of the environment often has been compromised. International organizations and businesses have been accused of putting corporate interests and profits above environmental standards.

A portion of the U.S. Clean Air Act required both domestic and foreign producers to create a cleaner gasoline. Yet the World Trade Organization (WTO) ruled against the act. It stated that the act hindered free trade.

The WTO has made similar rulings in the past that favor free trade over the environment. For example, the U.S. Endangered Species Act requires that any shrimp sold in the United States must be caught using a Turtle Excluder Device (TED) that allows sea turtles to escape the net. However, the WTO does not require that the device be used. The WTO says that TEDs limit free trade. India and Pakistan continue to fish without TEDs.

"One reason why environmental protection is lagging in many countries is low incomes. . . . If poverty is at the core of the problem, economic growth will be part of the solution, to the extent that it allows countries to shift gears from more immediate concerns to long run sustainability issues."[2]

—*World Trade Organization*

More countries are becoming wealthier through increased international trade, new businesses, highways, airports, and other structures that expand the urban landscape. This expansion takes over the natural environment.

As countries grow industrially, air and water pollution increase. However, once a country achieves a certain level of economic wealth, environmental standards and regulations increase. In this way, expansion benefits the environment. John A. Charles, an environmental policy director at Cascade Policy Institutes, states,

. . . economic growth is bad for air and water pollution at the initial stages of industrialization, but later on reduces pollution as countries become rich enough to pay for control technologies. . . . The richer people become, the more they tend to value environmental objectives such as safe drinking water, proper sewage disposal, and clean air.[1]

AIDS patients in Africa have a difficult time affording medication.

Charles argues that the United States has become more efficient and less pollutant over time. The United States is now able to produce the same amount of economic output that it did 60 years ago, using only half as much energy.

CLIMATE AND DISEASE

Many industrialized countries have high environmental standards. Most developing nations simply cannot afford to meet these standards. As their countries continue to grow, more pollutants fill the air. This adds to the already large amount of pollution produced by developed nations. Pollutants are a major contributing factor to climate change and global warming. As the earth warms, there will be more floods, rain, and heat.

Globalization's effects on the climate have led to the increasing amount of heat-related deaths. Illnesses caused by polluted water from flooding and malnutrition also have increased. The large amounts of rainfall caused by climate change have increased the mosquito population. Mosquitoes carry the often-fatal disease malaria that infects millions of people worldwide.

"The transformation of virgin forests, pristine rivers, etc. into 're-sources' is simply not sustainable. . . . Corporate globalization, with its mandate to put profit first, above both planet and people, has pushed the life support systems of the Earth to the brink of collapse."[3]

— *Paul Wolfowitz, World Bank*

Worldwide Health

Many international organizations have put economic concerns above health concerns in developing countries. This could have a negative impact on a nation's long-term health.

Yet the increased connectedness of the global population has improved the health of billions. Many developing countries have greatly benefited. Vaccination programs have virtually eradicated diseases such as polio. A vitamin A supplement distributed in poverty-stricken areas has saved millions of children from a disease that causes night blindness.

The health of those within developing countries is largely affected by the food industry. Industrial farming has taken away the small family farm. Many people in the developing world rely upon small farms as their source of income. The industrial

Drug Resistance

In the early half of the twentieth century, diseases such as tuberculosis (TB) often caused massive and fatal outbreaks. This was especially common in highly populated areas. As better treatments became available, the occurrences of many of these diseases greatly decreased. Over the years, some of these diseases have become drug-resistant due to the widespread use of antibiotics. Doctors fear this could create a serious global health threat. The medical community would have a difficult time keeping up with effective medicines to treat patients infected with the drug-resistant strains.

Resistant strains of TB have become increasingly common, especially in Eastern Europe. In Russia's prisons, as many as 20 percent of those infected with TB are infected with a strain that cannot be treated with current antibiotics. Due to the increased movement of people caused by globalization, drug-resistant TB could easily spread to other areas at a rapid rate. In 1992, New York City faced a small outbreak of the disease that eventually led to 500 deaths and about $750 million spent to contain it.

farming system buys up small farms and merges them into giant ones. In the process, crop diversity is eliminated. The Food and Agriculture Organization (FAO) and the United Nations (UN) estimate that the world has already lost nearly 75 percent of crop diversity due to industrial farming. In addition, developing nations do not always have the same food safety standards. Exported food could carry diseases. Also, many of the products from developing nations are exposed to pesticides that the developed world has banned. Yet these products are being exported by developing countries. Farmworkers and consumers are exposed to dangerous chemicals in the process.

However, without an international trade system, food would be more expensive and localized. Cold climates would not have access to most fruits or vegetables for at least half of the year. This could contribute to vitamin deficiencies and malnutrition. In addition, opening up developing countries to the international food industry could raise their economic development. ⌐

*Patients suffering from tuberculosis are treated
in a hospital in Hyderabad, India.*

Sesame Street *muppet Elmo wears a Muslim hat in a classroom in Malaysia.*

CULTURE

The spread of globalization impacts almost every aspect of life. Culture, the basis for civilization, is greatly influenced by it. Its impact on culture can be beneficial, leading to diversity and innovation. Its impact can also force individual cultures to conform to the values and traditions of dominant countries.

Every day, children in 120 countries worldwide tune in to the popular children's television show Sesame Street. In Russia it is called Ulitsa Sezam. In Egypt, it is known as Alam SimSim. And in China, viewers know it as Shima Jie. This American classic has gained worldwide recognition and helps children everywhere learn critical tools and values at an early age. But while Sesame Street is originally an American creation, it has diversified in a way to fit each unique society's culture. For example, in China, instead of the alphabet, children learn the meaning and origin of different Chinese characters. The Chinese version also promotes traditional family values, such as respect and devotion to one's elders. In South Africa, where HIV/AIDS is a serious problem, a muppet living with HIV teaches children about the disease. It also helps to remove negative ideas about people living with HIV. In the Palestinian region, where violence and conflict have plagued the area

Values in India

A law was passed in India making it illegal for children to neglect their elderly parents in their old age. Those found guilty could spend up to a month in jail. As India becomes increasingly modern and more globalized, some politicians fear traditional family values are eroding, such as living with extended family and taking care of one's elders.

"But while globalization has made it easier than ever to explore exotic destinations, it has also exacted a price: generic creep. As the world becomes smaller, mega-corporations extend their reach and begin to intrude on local businesses and culture. . . . From Singapore to Switzerland, you can get coffee at Starbucks and a burger and fries at McDonald's. Coke and Pepsi are available in the peaks of the Himalayas and the depths of the Amazon jungle."[2]

—John Rosenthal,
culture writer

for decades, children watch characters who teach acceptance, friendship, and the value of others' differences.

Through advancements in free trade, technology, communication, and transportation, cross-cultural interaction is increasing. This can lead to greater cultural diversity. People exposed to foreign cultures may bring aspects of those cultures into their own lives. Economist Philippe Legrain argues,

The beauty of globalization is that it can free people from the tyranny of geography. Just because someone was born in France does not mean they can only aspire to speak French, eat French food, read French books, and so on. . . . That we are increasingly free to choose our cultural experiences enriches our lives immeasurably. We could not always enjoy the best the world has to offer.[1]

AMERICANIZATION

The United States is criticized for exporting "mass-produced products of popular culture."[3]

A McDonald's restaurant in Pakistan

Worldwide, people have protested globalization as leading to an "Americanization" of the world's cultures. The United States has a dominant role in international organizations and influence on trade. Therefore, the United States can impose its values and its products onto other countries. Meic Pearse, author of *Why the Rest Hates the West*, writes,

> *Very many, especially Third World, people have the sensation that everything they hold dear and sacred is being rolled over by an economic and cultural juggernaut that doesn't even know it's doing it . . . and wouldn't understand why what it's destroying is important or of value.*[4]

Maintaining Cultural Identity

Although the United States has a large media industry, other countries are drawn to their own products, instead of U.S. products. People in Germany watch more German-produced television shows. India has created its own film industry, nicknamed Bollywood. Although it is smaller than Hollywood, it remains extremely popular. Thomas L. Friedman, *New York Times* foreign affairs columnist, commented,

---

McDonald's

Approximately every six hours a new McDonald's restaurant opens up somewhere in the world. As of 2008, McDonald's has as many as 30,000 restaurants in more than 119 countries. While many see McDonald's as American as apple pie, the franchise has gone to great lengths to promote a culturally diverse image. In India, McDonald's offers two separate menus. One menu is for the Muslim population that does not eat pork, and another menu is for the Hindu population that does not eat beef. Muslims can order Maharaja Macs, which are made of mutton. Hindus may order a vegetarian McAloo Tikki burger. From McLak burgers in Norway to teriyaki ones in Japan, McDonald's has attempted to customize its menu in almost every country to fit the local population's eating habits.

While McDonald's may not be a perfect example of globalization, it has brought some positive changes. For example, in certain traditional Muslim cultures, women often meet at McDonald's. It is viewed as an acceptable place for a woman to be alone. McDonald's has also raised sanitary standards in some areas. People started demanding that local restaurants match the cleaning standards of the franchise. In each culture that McDonald's has entered, its role has changed based on that culture's needs and priorities.

I think that it [Americanization] was true to a point, and it was certainly true early on, but it's less and less true every day. . . . And I look at the internet, which is now so much of a driver of globalization, as like a big pizza that every society basically puts its own local culture on. . . . It will be sometime near 2010, where there will be more Chinese and Indian internet users than there are Americans. And that's going to change the flavor of the internet pizza. So, yes, initially America was the driver of this system and dominated in the cultural sense, but I think that will be less and less true with every passing day.[5]

As globalization gains a stronger hold, many countries have become more nationalistic. They reject Western values. Some countries, such as Saudi Arabia, Iran, and North Korea, have gone to great lengths to limit Western influence. However, this rejection of most everything "West" creates tension between fundamentalists, as they are often called, and those from developed nations.

Other nations have not entirely closed themselves off to Western influence. But more countries are promoting their own values and traditions while still retaining open markets and other Western concepts. Politicians and government officials in some Asian

Whaling Ban

At a United Nations (UN) conference in the spring of 2000, both Japan and Norway sought exemption from the international whaling ban. They said that the ban interfered with their cultural heritage of hunting whales. The whales that these two countries hunted were not endangered. They argued that there was no reason for a ban. Both countries insisted that the ban needlessly harmed their local fishing communities and traditional ways of life. However, the United States and many other UN member countries disagreed. They sought to impose trading restrictions on Japan and Norway if they continued to hunt whales.

countries are promoting Asian values. These values focus on the community. They also reflect hard work, respect for authority, and social discipline. Much of the economic success in Asia over the past two decades has been attributed to their promotion of national values. This is a great example of how globalization and cultural identity can coexist.

As anthropologist James Watson said, "Culture is a set of ideas, reactions, and expectations that is constantly changing as people and groups themselves change."[6]

A Tibetan boy wears traditional dress at a globalization protest.

TIMELINE

114 BCE	1492	1700s
Trade route known as the Silk Road is established in Europe and Asia.	The rediscovery of the Americas leads to increased trading.	The Industrial Revolution begins. Trade increases dramatically.

1930s	1937	1939
The U.S. economy experiences problems. The Great Depression begins and impacts other countries as well.	Sino-Japanese War begins.	World War II begins in Europe.

1914

World War I begins. Most industrialized countries put up protectionist barriers on international trade, hurting many countries' economies.

1918

World War I ends. The United States takes on a dominant international role.

1920s

The U.S. economy thrives; however, many protectionist trade barriers are still in place internationally.

1944

Leaders from many of the industrialized countries form the Bretton Woods agreement to establish a liberal international economic system.

1945

World War II ends. The Cold War begins.

1945

The International Monetary Fund (IMF) is ratified on December 27.

TIMELINE

1948	1992	1993
Members of the United Nations (UN) General Assembly draft the Universal Declaration of Human Rights in December.	A massive outbreak of drug-resistant tuberculosis (TB) hits New York City.	Approximately 500 million people board airplanes for international flights.

2000	2001
UN Millennium Development Goals are agreed upon.	The Doha Development Round begins in November.

1995

The World Trade Organization (WTO) is formed through negotiations known as the Uruguay Round.

1999

From November 26 to December 6, protesters gather in downtown Seattle, Washington, to protest a WTO meeting.

2000

Approximately 1.4 billion people board airplanes for international flights.

2002

On May 3, Occidental Petroleum withdraws its plans to drill for oil on U'wa tribal land.

2008

Some countries consider boycotting the Olympic Games to protest China's human rights violations.

ESSENTIAL FACTS

AT ISSUE

Opposed

❖ Globalization is a means by which developed countries exploit developing nations through free trade agreements.

❖ Globalization causes the Westernization, or Americanization, of the world, where Western and U.S. influences overtake traditional identities.

❖ Globalization exploits workers with meager wages and poor working conditions and has damaging effects on the environment.

❖ Globalization has increased the gap between the rich and the poor—both within nations and between developed and developing countries.

In Favor

❖ Globalization is a means by which countries may develop economically and increase their standard of living.

❖ International trade increases economic wealth and establishes good political relations with other trading partners.

❖ Globalization increases jobs and allows for more efficient uses of resources, which helps the environment in the long run.

❖ Globalization can reduce poverty, give developing nations a chance to grow economically, and be used as a tool to advance civil liberties, democracy, and human rights throughout the world.

CRITICAL DATES

1944
Leaders from many of the industrialized countries came together to form the Bretton Woods agreement. They hoped to establish a liberal international economic system.

1945
The International Monetary Fund (IMF) was ratified.

1995
The World Trade Organization (WTO) was formed through a series of negotiations called the Uruguay Round.

1999
From November 26 to December 6, protesters gathered in downtown Seattle, Washington, to protest against a WTO meeting being held in the city.

2001
The Doha Development Round began in November 2001.

QUOTES

"Globalization is a set of beliefs that fosters a sense of connectivity, interdependence, and integration in the world community. It highlights commonalities without overlooking differences, and it extends benefits and responsibilities on a global scale."—*Abbas J. Ali, professor and executive director of the American Society for Competitiveness*

"The policies of economic globalization . . . concentrate wealth at the top, removing from governments and communities the very tools needed to ensure equity and to protect workers, social services, the environment, and sustainable livelihoods. In this way, economic globalization and its institutions—including the International Monetary Fund (IMF), the World Bank, the World Trade Organization . . . have created the most dramatic increase in global inequality . . . and have increased global poverty."—*Antonia Juhasz, project director of the International Forum on Globalization*

ADDITIONAL RESOURCES

SELECT BIBLIOGRAPHY

Gerdes, Louise I. *Globalization*. Opposing Viewpoints Series. Farmington Hills, MI: Greenhaven Press, 2006.

Giddens, Anthony. *Runaway World: How Globalization Is Reshaping Our Lives*. New York: Routledge, 2000.

Mandelbaum, Michael. *The Ideas That Conquered the World: Peace, Democracy, and Free Markets in the Twenty-first Century*. New York: PublicAffairs, 2002.

Stiglitz, Joseph E. *Globalization and Its Discontents*. New York: W.W. Norton & Co., 2002.

Thomas, Janet. *The Battle in Seattle: The Story Behind and Beyond the WTO Demonstrations*. Golden, CO: Fulcrum Publishing, 2000.

FURTHER READING

Frost, Randall, and Tina Schwartzenberger. *Globalization and Trade*. North Mankato, MN: Smart Apple Media, 2004.

Gerdes, Louise I. *Globalization*. Opposing Viewpoints Series. Farmington Hills, MI: Greenhaven Press, 2006.

Nelson, Sheila. *UN and Cultural Globalization: One World, Many People*. Philadelphia, PA: Mason Crest Publishers, 2007.

WEB LINKS

To learn more about globalization, visit ABDO Publishing Company on the World Wide Web at **www.abdopublishing.com**. Web sites about globalization are featured on our Book Links page. These links are routinely monitored and updated to provide the most current information available.

For More Information

For more information on this subject, contact or visit the following organizations.

Centre for Research on Globalization
PO Box 55019
11 Notre-Dame Ouest
Montreal, Qc
H2Y 4A7
Canada
www.globalresearch.ca
The Centre for Research on Globalization is a nonprofit organization based in Canada. The organization is an independent research and media group providing research and analysis of international issues.

The World Bank
1818 H Street, NW
Washington, DC 20433
USA
(202) 473-1000
www.worldbank.org
The World Bank provides financial assistance to developing nations.

World Trade Organization
Centre William Rappard
Rue de Lausanne 154
CH-1211 Geneva 21
Switzerland
(41-22) 739 51 11
www.wto.int
The World Trade Organization is an international organization that attempts to regulate trade between nations.

Glossary

abolish
> To put an end to something.

capitalism
> An economic system in which the means of production are privately owned and it is governed by the principles of a free-market economy of supply and demand.

Cold War
> The period between 1945 and 1989 that was characterized by a conflict between the Soviet-led East and the United States-led West over ideological differences.

communism
> An ideology pursuing a classless society based on the common ownership of the means of production.

democracy
> A government in which citizens exercise power by voting and electing leaders to represent them.

developing nation
> A poor country that is trying to become economically advanced.

disarmament
> Reducing the size and strength of a country's armed forces; giving up weapons.

economy
> A country's wealth and resources in relation to its production, distribution, and consumption of goods and services.

exploit
> To treat unfairly or use someone or something for personal gain.

export
> Goods that are produced in one country and sold in a different country.

free trade
> Trade between two countries that do not impose restrictive trade barriers on one another.

fundamentalism
　An attitude that stresses a strict adherence to basic or traditional values.

guerrilla warfare
　Revolutionary efforts led by citizens against a government, usually with tactics of sabotage and small-scale combat.

import
　Goods that come from another country.

indigenous
　Originating in or characteristic of a particular place or country.

industrialization
　The adoption of industrial methods of production and manufacturing.

outsource
　To purchase international goods or services rather than using local ones.

privatize
　To transfer ownership or control of something from the public to a private industry.

protectionism
　Trade barriers put into place by a country to protect certain industries from global competition.

proxy war
　A war not fought by the principal opponents but by third parties.

recession
　A decline in the economy.

sanction
　An action taken by one country to make another country act a certain way.

subsidy
　Monetary assistance given to private sectors by the government.

Glossary Continued

sweatshop
A factory where laborers usually work long hours in unsafe or uncomfortable conditions and generally earn little pay.

tariff
A fee placed on traded goods.

terrorism
The systematic use of violent tactics often employed to bring attention to a certain group's demands.

totalitarian
A government or regime that enforces strict control over its citizens.

treaty
An agreement made between two or more governments.

tuberculosis
An infection that affects a person's lungs.

U'wa
An indigenous tribe from Colombia.

Source Notes

Chapter 1. What Is Globalization?
1. "Tribe's Suicide Pact." 24 Apr. 2008. <http://www.vhemt.org/uwa.htm>.
2. Ibid.
3. "Local Cultures." Occidental Oil Web site. <http://www.oxy.com/Social%20Responsibility/rights/local_cult.htm>.
4. Louise I. Gerdes. *Globalization.* Opposing Viewpoints Series. Farmington Hills, MI: Greenhaven Press, 2006. 21.

Chapter 2. The Origins of Globalization
None.

Chapter 3. International Organizations
1. Cordell Hull. *The Memoirs of Cordell Hull.* New York: MacMillan, 1948. 81.
2. Joseph E. Stiglitz. *Globalization and Its Discontents.* New York: W.W. Norton & Co., 2002. 17–18.
3. Janet Thomas. *The Battle in Seattle: The Story Behind and Beyond the WTO Demonstrations.* Golden, CO: Fulcrum Publishing, 2000. 53.

Chapter 4. The Developing World
1. Erla Zwingle. "A World Together." National Geographic. 24 Apr. 2008. <http://www.nationalgeographic.com/xpeditions/activities/11/popup/article.html>.
2. "Terrorism May Have Put Sand in Its Gear but Globalization Won't Stop." YaleGlobal Online. <http://yaleglobal.yale.edu/>.

Chapter 5. The Developed World
1. Anthony Giddens. *Runaway World: How Globalization Is Reshaping Our Lives.* New York: Routledge, 2000. 60–61.
2. Louise I. Gerdes. *Globalization.* Opposing Viewpoints Series. Farmington Hills, MI: Greenhaven Press, 2006. 178.

Chapter 6. Migration
1. "How Are Illegal Immigration and Globalization Related." *Immigration: Pros and Cons.* 20 Jan. 2008.
2. Ibid.

Source Notes Continued

Chapter 7. International Stability

1. Louise I. Gerdes. *Globalization.* Opposing Viewpoints Series. Farmington Hills, MI: Greenhaven Press, 2006. 50.
2. Michael Mandelbaum. *The Ideas That Conquered the World: Peace, Democracy, and Free Markets in the Twenty-first Century.* New York: PublicAffairs, 2002. 239.
3. Anthony Giddens. *Runaway World: How Globalization Is Reshaping Our Lives.* New York: Routledge, 2000. 31.
4. "10 Benefits of the WTO Trading System." World Trade Organization. 24 Apr. 2008. <http://www.wto.org/english/res_e/doload_e/10b_e.pdf>.
5. Erla Zwingle. "A World Together." National Geographic. 24 Apr. 2008. <http://www.nationalgeographic.com/xpeditions/activities/11/popup/article.html>.
6. Louise I. Gerdes. *Globalization.* Opposing Viewpoints Series. Farmington Hills, MI: Greenhaven Press, 2006. 74.
7. Ibid. 79.

Chapter 8. Human Rights

1. *Universal Declaration of Human Rights.* United Nations. 24 Apr. 2008. <http://www.un.org/Overview/rights.html>.
2. Erla Zwingle. "A World Together." National Geographic. 24 Apr. 2008. <http://www.nationalgeographic.com/xpeditions/activities/11/popup/article.html>.
3. Louise I. Gerdes. *Globalization.* Opposing Viewpoints Series. Farmington Hills, MI: Greenhaven Press, 2006. 117.
4. Janet Thomas. *The Battle in Seattle: The Story Behind and Beyond the WTO Demonstrations.* Golden, CO: Fulcrum Publishing, 2000. 78.

Chapter 9. Health and the Environment

1. Louise I. Gerdes. *Globalization.* Opposing Viewpoints Series. Farmington Hills, MI: Greenhaven Press, 2006. 94.
2. Ibid. 94.
3. Ibid. 88.
4. "UNICEF: Child health improves, work remains." 10 Dec. 2007. <http://www.msnbc.msn.com/id/22182565/>.

Chapter 10. Culture
1. Louise I. Gerdes. *Globalization*. Opposing Viewpoints Series. Farmington Hills, MI: Greenhaven Press, 2006. 35.
2. "If This Is Tuesday, This Must Be the Hard Rock Paris." msn. com. 29 Oct. 2007. <http://travel.msn.com/Guides/article. aspx?cp-documentid=428393>.
3. Louise I. Gerdes. *Globalization*. Opposing Viewpoints Series. Farmington Hills, MI: Greenhaven Press, 2006. 44.
4. Meic Pearse. *Why the Rest Hates the West*. Downers Grove, IL: InterVarsity Press, 2004. 35.
5. "Terrorism May Have Put Sand in Its Gear but Globalization Won't Stop." YaleGlobal Online. 24 Apr. 2008. <http://yaleglobal.yale.edu/>.
6. James Watson. *Golden Arches East: McDonald's in East Asia.* Stanford, CA: Stanford University Press, 1997. 8.

INDEX

Industrial Revolution, 20–23, 57
industrialized nations. *See* developed nations
industrializing nations. *See* developing nations
international corporations, 13–15, 35, 36, 43, 69, 70, 75–77, 81
International Monetary Fund, 30, 31–34, 40, 77, 78
international stability, 52, 57, 64–70

Japan, 34, 42, 92, 94

malaria, 46, 84
Malawi, 60, 61–62
McDonald's, 92

North American Free Trade Agreement, 59

Occidental, 7–11
outsourcing, 49–51

Pew Global Attitudes Project, 13, 42–43
pollution, 82–84
poverty, 14, 29, 33–34, 46, 55–56, 58, 70, 76–78, 82, 85
protectionism, 42, 51–52

remittance, 60
Russia, 25, 67, 69, 85, 88

Saudi Arabia, 42–45, 93
Seattle protest, 28–30, 36–37
Senegal, 54–55
Sesame Street, 88–89
Shell, 7–9, 11
Silk Road, 19
Somalia, 60–61, 63

terrorism, 13, 68, 70
trade barriers, 22, 24, 26, 31–35, 41–42, 44, 46, 51, 52, 59
tuberculosis, 85, 87

Ukraine, 74
United Nations, 45, 72, 74, 86, 94
  Millennium Goals, 45–46
Universal Declaration of Human Rights, 72–73
U.S. Clean Air Act, 81
U'wa, 6–10

Westernization, 14. *See also* Americanization
workers' rights, 14, 43, 75–78, 86
  sweatshops, 76
World Bank, 29–34, 40, 78, 84
World Trade Organization, 29–30, 35–36, 42, 48, 52, 69, 76, 81
World War I, 23–24, 30, 57
World War II, 24–25, 30, 57, 72

About the Author

Sara Hamilton received a Bachelor of Arts degree in English literature from Minnesota State University, Mankato. She has recently served as lead editor for two children's educational books. In her spare time, Sara enjoys traveling, cooking, and lounging around with her pet rabbit, Norma.

Photo Credits

Richard Vogel/AP Images, cover, 3; Ariana Cubillos/AP Images, 6; AP Images, 11, 24, 27, 97, 99 (bottom); Ben Margot/AP Images, 17; Eric Draper/AP Images, 28; Itsu Inouye/AP Images, 37, 99 (top); Vincent Yu/AP Images, 38; Esteban Felix/AP Images, 47; Ben Curtis/AP Images, 48; Sayyid Azim/AP Images, 63; Donald Stampfli/AP Images, 71, 72; Anat Givon/AP Images, 75; Denis Farrell/AP Images, 80, 98; Saurabh Das/AP Images, 83; Marhesh Kumar A/AP Images, 87; Andy Wong/AP Images, 88; K. M. Chaudary/AP Images, 91; Manish Swarup/AP Images, 95; © North Wind / North Wind Picture Archives, 18, 21, 96; Wikipedia, 32; AFP / Getty Images, 41, 54, 60, 64; Getty Images, 53, 79